Professor Birdsong's 117 Dumbest Criminal Stories: The Southwest

Leonard Birdsong

Winghurst Publications

*Professor Birdsong's 117 Dumbest Criminal Stories:
The Southwest* by Leonard Birdsong
© 2015 Leonard Birdsong
ISBN: 978-0-9898452-6-7

Winghurst Publications
1969 S. Alafaya Trail / Suite 303
Orlando, FL 32828-8732
www.BirdsongsLaw.com
lbirdsong@barry.edu

Disclaimer:
The facts that are recounted in the stories in this volume are true
and in the public domain, as best as Professor Birdsong can
determine from his research of court documents, newspapers,
and wire services. The author's commentaries on these stories
are his own views and opinions and do not reflect the official
policy or position of any Law school, Law firm or other
organization with which the author may be affiliated. The
opinions provided herein are not intended to malign or defame
any religion, ethnic group, club, organization, company,
individual or anyone or anything. The author further covenants
and represents that the work contains no matter that will incite
prejudice, amount to an invasion of privacy, be libelous,
obscene or otherwise unlawful or which infringe upon any
proprietary interest at common law, trademark, trade secret,
patent or copyright. The author is the sole proprietor of the work
and all parts thereof.

Permissions:
Cover graphics:
© Ievgen Melamud | Dreamstime.com
© Liusa | Dreamstime.com (x2)
© Dayzeren | Dreamstime.com

Book cover design: Rik Feeney / **www.RickFeeney.com**

Table of Contents

Introduction

Law Professor Leonard Birdsong lives in Orlando, Florida where he teaches Criminal Law, Evidence, and Immigration Law. He has written many scholarly legal pieces since joining the legal academy.

Among his scholarly pieces are his articles entitled: The Formation of The Caribbean Court of Justice: The Sunset of British Colonial Rule in the English Speaking Caribbean and The Felony Murder Doctrine Revisited: A Proposal for Calibrating Punishment that Reaffirms the Sanctity of Human Life of Co-Felons Who Are Victims.

This is not one of those scholarly pieces!

⌘

This volume of *Professor Birdsong's 117 Dumbest Criminal Stories: Southwest* is written just for fun and enjoyment. It showcases the kind of many funny and weird criminal law stories that he has found and written about since 2010. The stories in this volume come to you from the states of Arizona, California, New Mexico, and Texas -- the Southwest region of the U.S. Read them, some will make you laugh out loud some will make you chuckle. Go ahead and laugh or chuckle at these stories and then go to Amazon.com and chose from his other inexpensive humor books for more such laughs. There are two series: Professor Birdsong's Dumbest Criminal Stories and Professor Birdsong's Weird Criminal Law Stories. As a matter of fact, you may find all of these other volumes at Amazon.com or by going to his website: LeonardBirdsong.com.

Some of you may criticize Professor Birdsong's editing of several of the stories that appear here, but be aware Professor Birdsong attempts to report the stories herein as they appeared in police reports and news reports that appeared in the public domain without changing the original story.

Enjoy the stories herein and have a few good laughs.

Chapter One

Drunken and/or disorderly Dummies from the Southwest

TEXAS: *Oh really... "Affluenza?" Come on!* Recently, a judge handed down a sentence of probation and no jail time for a teenage drunken driver who killed four pedestrians. The Fort Worth judge accepted the defense lawyer's arguments that the 16-year-old, Ethan Couch, suffers from "affluenza" and has no self-control because his rich parents let him drink with no consequences. According to reports, he will be on probation for ten years.

TEXAS: *Not a stiff sentence but maybe he will be shamed into sobriety.* A judge ordered a drunken driver, who served 90 days in jail, for killing a man in a crash to spend four consecutive Saturdays at the crash scene in suburban Houston wearing a sign that read: "I killed Aaron Coy Pennywell while driving drunk." Michael Giancona, 38, must also hang a picture taken at the scene of the 2011 crash in his living room.

CALIFORNIA: *A cross cross-dresser on a rampage? Why?* A man in a leopard print bikini top and black skirt rampaged through a San Diego Denny's restaurant earlier this year, sending patrons scurrying as he hurled glasses, a skillet and utensils. It was revealed that the cross cross-dresser, who thought his cell phone had been stolen, went on the rampage when a manager turned down his request to check the restaurant surveillance footage. Police were called, but there is no information whether an arrest was made.

TEXAS: *Yes Adam, life can be a "drag" if you let it...*Recently a convicted sex offender, Adam Mabery, just released from prison allegedly broke into a Goodwill Thrift Store in the town of Sherman and modeled a red dress, purse and heels. Surveillance cameras recorded the intoxicated Mabery dancing and bleeding from the broken glass around the store.

TEXAS: *What a naked loser...Ewww... Do you think they'll still sell those garments?* A buck-naked driver caused a commotion when he smashed his pickup truck through the front entrance doors of the Southwest Center Mall in Dallas. He emerged from the damaged vehicle, walked over to the Champs Sports outlet and started donning clothes from the rack until police arrived and nabbed him.

CALIFORNIA: *Robbins – You are a blockhead!* The fellow who, as a child, voiced the voice of the peanuts cartoon character, Charlie Brown, threatened to kill a West coast plastic surgeon because he didn't like the breasts the doctor put on his ex-girlfriend. Peter Robbins, 57, voiced Charlie Brown in classic TV shows like the "Christmas Story" and "Great Pumpkin" specials for five years. Police report that Robbins left dozens of threatening handwritten screeds and voice messages for Dr. Lori Saltz.

ARIZONA: *There must be no canoodling in school…* A principal of a charter school was forced to resign and his secretary was fired after a 16-year-old student used her smart phone to make a video of the two making out. We learn further that the video by 16-year- old Myranda Garber at the school in the town of Quartzsite caused a scandal because both the principal and the secretary have spouses.

CALIFORNIA: *Can we say the police jumped the gun?* Lorenzo Oliver, 54, was arrested and taken to jail for attacking a possum in his back yard, after the possum went after his dogs. Oliver has now been cleared of all charges and he has also been cleared to sue the Anaheim Police Department – because it is not against the law to kill possums in California.

CALIFORNIA: *What a dangerous idiot. We never knew that snakes let off a smell!* A teacher who was arrested a few months ago for hoarding more than 400 hundred snakes in his Orange County home has now been charged with felony animal abuse. William Beckman was arrested after neighbors complained about a foul smell coming from his home.

ARIZONA: *Why not arrest him for adultery or for being stupid?* Stephen Chapman, 22, of Pinal County, was found in bed with a wayward spouse. When her husband showed up Chapman refused to leave the couple's home. It is reported that Chapman allegedly charged at the shotgun toting husband, who then shot his wife's lover in the hand. However, when police showed up at the house it was Chapman who was arrested, on suspicion of disorderly conduct.

ARIZONA: *OK, ok, some states have just become ridiculous with their anti-alcohol campaigns.* Police on underage drinking patrol singled out a father at a Cardinals NFL preseason football game that had his fifteen-year-old son to hold his beer while the father took photographs of the action on the field. The police officers kicked the whole family out of the stadium, and state liquor officials said that if they had been stricter, the father could have received two years in jail.

NEW MEXICO: *Absolut or Cristal?* A mother in Albuquerque was caught while trying to shoplift a bottle of vodka while pushing her 1-year-old in its stroller. Grocery store employees caught Andrea Garcia as she allegedly tried to secret the vodka into the stroller with the baby. Her boyfriend threatened the employees with a knife and then ran off and abandoned his child and its mother, according a police report.

NEW MEXICO: *Bet they saw he's "nuts" on that flight.* A passenger stripped naked during a US Airways flight and resisted efforts to cover him with a blanket before two off duty law enforcement officers on board subdued and handcuffed him. Keith Wright, 50, of Bronx, New York, was taken into custody after he disrobed while sitting in his seat at the back of the plane. The plane was carrying 150 passengers from Charlotte to L.A. Wright punched and kicked the flight attendant who tried to cover him with a blanket. She sought assistance from the off duty officers. After landing in Albuquerque, Wright told the FBI he suffers from bipolar disorder and had not taken his medication before leaving New York. Wright had no memory of the flight or his behavior on the plane.

NEW MEXICO: *There was certainly a "ceiling" to her intelligence...* A woman arrested and taken to a hospital for swallowing drugs, tried to escape custody by climbing through the hospital ceiling. She was missing for an hour before police found up there.

ARIZONA: *Appeal? Now we get it, "a peal" like in a bell....how smart...* Not even the house of the Lord shall be exempt from the city's noise code. A Phoenix church bishop got a 10 day suspended jail sentence because the tolling bells of the Cathedral of Christ the King were too loud, sparking complaints from neighbors. Bishop Richard Painter said he would appeal.

NEW MEXICO: *The boyfriend must have cheated on her and she found out about it!* A violent woman was arrested after police said she attacked her boyfriend with a boot, a tire iron and a screwdriver – while he was behind the wheel with the car moving. The Dona Ana County Sheriff's Office says the suspect was being held in jail on battery charges.

TEXAS: *Dude they weren't even going to send you to jail, why did you run?* A man who would have been sentenced to six months' probation for a petty crime got those 180 days behind bars instead when he fled custody at a Texas courthouse just before his sentencing. Making matters worse James Carroll led police on a car chase through three counties.

TEXAS: *WOOF*.... A Lewisville man, reportedly, went postal when one of his two dogs defecated in the house. We learn that Michael Stephens, 76, shot and killed his wife and both of his dogs upon finding the dog mess. He then held off police in a five hour standoff before he was arrested.

TEXAS: *Well, if you can't beat them – join them!* A police officer in San Antonio, Texas, was driving so recklessly while trying to pull people over that other officers stopped him and discovered he was stinking drunk. Lt. Arthur MacCubbin, 47, Deputy of the year in 2006, was charged with DWI and put on leave.

Chapter Two

Dumbest Criminal Robbers of the Southwest

TEXAS: *You think…..* Guess this fellow needed an energy boost for the night he had planned. A wheelchair bound robber ignored a cash register at a Dallas 7-Eleven, snatching 10 packets of condoms and an energy drink. Police said the suspect was probably drunk.

CALIFORNIA: *What kind of dummy brings his mail to a robbery?* A thief from the town of Hemet allegedly robbed a supermarket and threatened to shoot a security guard as he fled the store. Police later found that the suspect, Stallone Barr, had dropped a piece of mail with his address on it, and they didn't take long to track him down

TEXAS: *…Always say please and thank you and leave a tip!* Jesus Ventura, 37, appears to have been raised to have good manners. He allegedly robbed a Chase bank branch in Dallas and then slipped the teller $20 and said, "Here's a tip for you." Ventura, ran off but was stopped by an off duty fireman He was subsequently arrested and faces federal bank robbery charges.

CALIFORNIA: *Ninjas my foot…Bet this was an inside job!* There may be some truth to the rumor that Ninja marijuana bandits are on the loose in the suburbs of LA. A man delivering medical marijuana maintains he was robbed recently by two men dressed as ninjas in West Covinia. The delivery man said the ninjas took his pot and his cash.

ARIZONA: *And, we know he is not really an "Angel."* Sheriff' deputies in Arizona City arrested Angel Maza. He was arrested for allegedly burglarizing the home of a woman who had discovered him in her bedroom while armed with a handgun. Maza who is 36-years-old, told the arresting officers that the "devil" planted a stolen gun on him and forced him to go into the woman's house.

CALIFORNIA: *Yuk, yuk…A Judge with a sense of humor…* Baron Stein, an unemployed San Diego tow truck driver, admitted he was struggling to feed his family when he stole 1,000 pounds of avocados, worth $1,500. He confessed his crime and took a plea deal. He was given no jail time but as part of his probation he was ordered to possess no more than 10 avocados at any one time.

NEW MEXICO: *El Stupido y crudo, perhaps….* A clumsy burglar in Albuquerque was arrested after he tried to break into a college office and became tangled up in the venetian blinds as he crawled through a window. The accused burglar, Thomas Molina, who was allegedly trying to steal computers became so entangled that he had to be helped out of the blinds bind by police before being taken off to jail.

CALIFORNIA: *No sale!* A woman was arrested after she allegedly held up a bank during her test drive of a used car. The suspect told the seller riding with her that she just needed to pop in the bank and get some money. He didn't know how she got the cash until police surrounded them and arrested her.

TEXAS: *What honeynuts...* Thieves snatched a 500 pound beehive packed with 5,000 angry bees from outside a Houston restaurant which used the insects to make honey. Police say it may have been a "sting operation."

CALIFORNIA: *Dude, you're an idiot!* A San Diego bank robber broke a rule of robbery – don't flee the robbery with vanity plates on your auto. The alleged robber pulled a gun at a teller window and fled on foot with $3,000. Witnesses advised police they saw him climb into a white Ford Expedition with the personalized license plate that read: ALM DUDE. The vehicle was registered to Robert Alm, 27, who was quickly arrested.

CALIFORNIA: *BURP!* An LA county Sheriff's deputy was arrested for allegedly smuggling heroin hidden in a bean and cheese burrito into the courthouse lockup. The deputy, Henry Marin, 27, pleaded not guilty to bringing drugs into a jail.

NEVADA: *Hiding a gun in a deep fryer is the craziest idea since paintball.* A man who attempted an armed robbery in the parking lot of a Las Vegas restaurant decided he had better get rid of the gun after the intended victims drove off. Expecting the law to arrive at any second, he tried to convince a waitress to hold the gun for him. Either the suspect or the waitress – police are not certain which – threw the gun into a deep fryer. The deep-fried gun exploded, but no one was hurt.

CALIFORNIA: *It could only have happened to a nincompoop!* A fleeing robber was arrested in Los Angeles after he jumped a fence at a baseball field and ran into several dozen police officers who were handing out Christmas toys to underprivileged children at the ball field.

CALIFORNIA: *Psssssst, Pssssssssssttt.....* A disabled grandmother, armed only with bear spray, told police she fended off 13 intruders who were after the medical marijuana she had growing in her back yard. The woman grabbed the spray and emptied the can on the "would be" thieves.

ARIZONA: *Boxers or Briefs??* A 20 year old Tempe man was caught at a pet shop stuffing two tarantulas down his pants before walking out. Authorities do not believe the crime was spontaneous because he had been seen in the store checking out the tanks previously by employees.

ARIZONA: *They have dubbed him the "beer baron of Arizona."* Anthony V, an 18-year-old teenager, was arrested in March in Phoenix for allegedly robbing 43 Circle K convenience stores and taking 233 12 packs of beer over eight months. The thefts reportedly totaled more than $5,000.

CALIFORNIA: *Doris you are too old for these kind of heists!* An 82 year old woman was arrested for allegedly committing five burglaries, in which she stole a total of $17,000 cash from El Segundo area doctors' offices. A frail Doris Gamble, who has been pulling burglaries since 1955 had to wear her hearing aid as the judge ordered her held in lieu of $250,000 bail.

ARIZONA: *Bet he was an ex-con who wanted to go back to jail...* Don't rob a bank when you're hungry. A man walked into a Yuma bank armed with a knife, threatened a teller, and walked out with an undisclosed amount of cash. He then decided to spend some of the money on beer and pizza at a restaurant just down the street from the bank. A suspicious police officer spotted him and made an arrest.

TEXAS: We hear that the Texas "panty robber" has struck again. For the last two years the "panty robber" has been breaking into East Texas homes and taking only women's undergarments. The Angelina

County Sheriff's Department recently reported the latest burglary wherein, for the first time, the "panty robber" also took children's underwear. Yep, there's a pervert on the loose in East Texas!

ARIZONA: *Why not! Cleanliness is next to godliness....* Police authorities in Eloy said that in two recent burglaries, the thieves first cleaned out the homes they had broken into and then they cleaned themselves up by taking showers before leaving.

NEW MEXICO: *Wacko Christo!* A man was arrested in Albuquerque after he carjacked an ambulance in the nude. The parents of Christopher Halverson, 27, called the police and an ambulance, believing their son was having a drug induced psychotic breakdown. Halverson jumped in the front seat of the ambulance, pushed the driver out of the way and took off. He crashed the ambulance a block and a half later.

TEXAS: *MTD – Much too dumb!* A thief was arrested in Houston after he tried to steal the hubcaps from a Cadillac parked outside a restaurant where sheriff's deputies were hosting a retirement party. After one of the deputies spotted the crime in progress the suspect was confronted by 30 law enforcement officials and promptly arrested. D'Oh!

NEW MEXICO: *You're a bad one Mr. Grinch!* A very bold thief towed away an offbeat pastor's "church on wheels," actually a trailer, from a parking lot in Albuquerque. The trailer contained $40,000 in equipment and toys for charity.

TEXAS: *Buzzards....* Police in Lewisville did not have to go to great lengths to arrest two men on felony theft charges. Why not? The crime took place at police headquarters. The suspects were in charge of the criminal evidence section at headquarters and over a three year period they, allegedly stole items, including tools, a knife, a camera, and thousands of dollars in cash.

NEW MEXICO: *Oh Poo...* Albuquerque police are trying to "flush" out brazen bathroom bandits who enter city restrooms and steal auto-flush sensor mechanisms. The thieves pose as plumbers, zero in on Flush-O-Matics and sell them for $30 each on the black market.

TEXAS: *Did they also take the pool water?* The summer of 2011 was really hot, especially in Richmond Hills where some thieves decided to steal a swimming pool. The thieves dismantled and carted away an above ground swimming pool from a family's back yard as temperatures reached 100 degrees.

TEXAS: *SCHMUCK!* A woman working at a Laredo liquor store took off her shoe and bashed an armed robber with her 7 inch stiletto heel. When other employees piled on him with their own makeshift weapons, the bandit ran for his life. He was soon caught and arrested by police.

TEXAS: *Idiot!* Nathan Pugh walked into a Dallas bank and demanded money from a teller, police report. The teller said she could not comply unless he showed her two forms of identification. He complied with the request. He was arrested a short time later.

TEXAS: *More stupid bank robbers! Real Dummies!* We learn that four people were just indicted in Houston for bank robbery after bragging about their $62,000 heist on Facebook. One of the suspects posted, "I'm Rich." another triumphantly posted, "Wipe my teeth with money."

TEXAS: *One weird family reunion... but we are mighty suspicious about it.* Stephanie Ramirez was working in a pizza parlor in Denton, when a robber wearing a wig and sunglasses barged in and demanded cash. As Rameriz took money from the register a coworker tackled the robber knocking off his disguise – and revealing that the robber was Ramirez's father. Police say they do not think that Rameriz herself was in on the robbery.

TEXAS: *Talk about getting your panties in a "bunch!"* A kinky thief walked into a Victoria's Secret in Dallas and made off with 130 pairs of panties valued at $1,067. Detectives are probing what styles of lustful lace the man fancied.

TEXAS: *Instead of a sub sounds like he got a "knuckle sandwich."* The wrong sub shop! A thief who attempted to rob a sub shop in Houston got a big surprise. As he jumped over the counter of the shop, the clerk punched him out. Customers then jumped in to Taser and handcuff the crook.

TEXAS: *We know, we know... He should have made a clean getaway. Ha, ha, ha, ha.* A man in Tyler called police to report that someone had kicked in the front door and broken into his home. The resident ran out and called the police. When they arrived, officers found the 25-year-old intruder taking a bath.

CALIFORNIA: *Times are hard all over folks...The headline read: "California Cops extinguish an odd crime spree."* A 45-year-old man was arrested for allegedly stealing 45 fire hydrants in Riverside and San Bernadino counties to sell for scrap metal, according to police. It's believed the thief posed as a repairman, unbolted the 80-100 pound hydrants, and hauled them away in broad daylight.

Chapter Three

The Most Bizarre Dumbest Criminals from the Southwest

ARIZONA: *Don't believe everything your family may tell you.* Law enforcement officials have egg on their faces after their spokeswoman learned that she was an undocumented alien living illegally in the U.S. Carmen Figueroa, who worked for 13 years as an officer and spokeswoman for the State Department of Public safety, resigned after her brother applied for a visa and underwent a background check that revealed his family's immigration status. Ms. Figueroa said her family had told her they had legally immigrated to the States. D'OH!

TEXAS: *This kind of foolishness even makes Rastafarian beliefs sound rational...* A Texas Tech student was allowed to wear a pasta strainer on his head for an official state ID card. Eddie Castillo convinced the Department of Public Safety he should be allowed to wear the strainer based on his religious freedom to worship the "Flying Spaghetti Monster." He stated further, that members of his "Pastafarian" church pray to the Flying Spaghetti Monster to advocate for greater separation between church and state.

TEXAS: *Could the headline have read..."Judge gets pissed off in the men's room!"* A man received a 30 day jail sentence for contempt of court after criticizing a judge in a courthouse men's room. State District Judge Jack Robinson ordered 69-year-old Don Bandelman released following two days in jail after a state appeals court in Austin made inquiries into the matter. Robinson had granted temporary custody of Bandelman's 13-year-old granddaughter to his son's ex-wife. Records reviewed by the Austin newspaper show Bandelman followed the judge into the men's room at the Caldwell County courthouse and berated him as "a fool" for his ruling.

TEXAS: *Fat chance he won't beat a Carrying a Pistol without License charge.* A 500-pound inmate was searched twice before he was sent off to the Harris County jail in Texas. But guards never found the gun he'd hidden under the flabs of his own flesh. The 25-year old man finally came clean to an officer before he was due to take a shower.

TEXAS: *It's a shame Johnny Cochrane is no longer with us. Maybe Matlock will represent him!* A man named Perry Mason was arrested in Houston for illegally trying to steer clients to a lawyer for legal services. Mason, who is not a lawyer, was charged with barratry -- a fancy way of calling him an ambulance chaser. Raymond Burr who played Perry Mason on TV, also could not be reached for comment -- as he died in 1993.

TEXAS: *How much does a frozen armadillo cost, anyway?* You don't hear about this kind of crime often. Police in Dallas are hunting for the man who attacked a woman with a frozen armadillo. The man was about to sell the iced carcass as food to the woman before they got into an argument over price. That's when he used the armadillo as a weapon and threw it at her. The 57 year old woman suffered bruises.

CALIFORNIA: *We believe he misses his "Mary Jane."* A marijuana farmer in Southern California has filed a lawsuit against his landlord because his marijuana crop was stolen from his residence. Ryan Avery is demanding $35,000. He might want to be careful with this suit, though. Police say that he is not a legal marijuana grower.

CALIFORNIA: *There's nothing like a hot cup of Joe in the morning!* A Crescent City supply store manager used his morning cup of coffee to ward off a hammer wielding masked intruder. As the would be thief ran at Chris Hegnes with his hammer raised and ready to strike, the quick witted worker threw his hot coffee in the man's face. The bandito fled.

TEXAS: *At least he did not have "Gin & Juice" with Snoop.* A state trooper has been reprimanded for posing for a photo with Snoop Dogg at the South by Southwest Festival in Austin because the rapper has several convictions for drug possession. Billy Spears was working security at the March 2015 event when Snoop Dogg asked to take a picture with him. The artist posted the image on Instagram with the comment, "Me n my deputy dogg." Department of Public Safety and Transportation officials saw the posting and cited Spears for deficiencies that require counselling by a supervisor. Spears's attorney says his client did not know about the rapper's criminal record. However, Spears can't appeal the citation because it isn't a formal disciplinary action.

ARIZONA: *If this program works, Tucson will become the new Dodge City!* A Tucson politician is raising money for a private program to hand out free shotguns to people in high crime neighborhoods. Sponsor Shaun McClusky plans to give people up to $400 to arm themselves and fight crime on their own. "Saying guns are responsible for killing people is like saying spoons are responsible for making people fat," said McClusky.

ARIZONA: *Dunce!* A convicted killer begged for mercy at his sentencing in Phoenix. He told the judge, "I regret every moment of the day I beat a 90 year old man to death." His family was by his side and he said that he planned to change his life and leave prison as a better man. Unfortunately, he then undermined his own case by turning around and flipping the finger to a television camera person. He received a 22 year sentence.

TEXAS: *Dummy!* A San Antonio man visited his son in jail and ended up behind bars himself. Jose Gonzalez, 53, thought it would be no problem to bring with him his combination walking cane and sword with him to the county jail. The cane passed through a metal detector, which went off, and guards unscrewed the top of it and found the two foot sword inside.

ARIZONA: *The grammar police got policed!* Two members of a group called the Typo Eradication Advancement League were arrested for defacing a historic, hand painted sign in the Grand Canyon by fixing grammatical errors on it. Both men were sentenced to a year's probation and cannot enter any national park. They must also pay $3,035 to repair the sign.

ARIZONA: *Who knew?* The Arizona Supreme Court has ruled that creating a tattoo is a form of protected speech. The Phoenix suburb of Mesa had denied Ryan and Laetitia Coleman a business permit for a tattoo parlor, prompting them to sue, claiming that their free speech rights were being violated. A lower court dismissed the suit, but the state's Supreme Court reinstated it. They ruled: "Recognizing that tattooing involves constitutionally protected speech, we hold that the Superior Court erred by dismissing the complaint as a matter of law."

TEXAS: *Sounds like a case of "selfie" incrimination.* Jailers have issued new charges against inmate Paul Reyes, 32, for allegedly possessing a contraband cell phone while locked up in the Bexar County. Sheriff's deputies received a tip that Reyes was taking pictures of himself behind bars and posting them to Facebook. Jailers found the phone in his pants and the charger around his waist.

TEXAS: *The headline read: "He is no rising star. But he was real 'pawn star.'"* Last February federal prosecutors obtained an indictment for William Keley, the disgraced former police chief of the town of Rising Star, Texas, for allegedly pawning $4 million worth of law enforcement equipment, including a machine gun.

TEXAS: *He who lives by the sword will...* Recently a Texas town opened the nation's largest luxury indoor shooting range.

On its opening day the range manager at the Frisco Gun Club shot himself in the hand while cleaning a weapon for a patron. He went to the hospital and, we learn that patrons went on with their shooting business at the club's 36 handgun-firing lanes, four rifle lanes and a VIP club.

TEXAS: *OK! You have been warned!!* Please be careful if you ever drive through the town of Missouri City. Why? The town has decided to charge a "crash tax" to motorist involved in accidents. The bill can run as high as $2,000 per wreck. The tax is meant to pay for emergency responders and only those drivers deemed responsible for collisions will be charged.

TEXAS: *It was her reputation for law abidingness that got hurt!* A Walmart worker was arrested in Houston after he allegedly followed a female shoplifting suspect out of the store, got in his car and ran over the suspect in the parking lot. The woman, who says she took nothing from the store, was not seriously hurt.

TEXAS: *The headline read: "What a Dumb-bass!"* A fisherman is in trouble after his bass catch exceeded the limit by 35, and he bragged about it on his blog. Dustin Heathman even allegedly posted photos of himself and his catch. This prompted 600 angry web responses as well as phone calls to gaming officials. Heathman now faces $17,500 in fines.

TEXAS: *Pepe Le Pew, maybe?* A woman shot at a skunk raiding her cats' food bowls on her porch – and hit her husband. The bullet ricocheted off the porch, went through the back door and struck her husband who was not seriously hurt. The husband and wife confirmed each other's stories, and even the skunk helped clear her. "He came back while our investigators were at the scene and tried to feed off the cat bowls," said Sheriff Christopher Kirk.

NEW MEXICO: *Nsane...police sans guns!* The small town of Vaughn has a small police department of two where neither of the officers is allowed to carry a gun because of legal problems. The chief lost his gun over a child support issue and his deputy can't carry a weapon because of a domestic violence incident. The chief said not having a gun was no problem, "We have Tasers, batons, mace…stuff like that," he said.

ARIZONA: *Wow that must have been some sexy, hot scene!* We learn that in February 2011, Tucson police finally captured the Arizona "techno-pirate" who had allegedly managed to insert a 37 second porno clip into a cable company's local telecast of the 2009 super Bowl. The so called, "flesh flash," forced Comcast to pay out $10 "we're sorry" refunds to 80,000 Tucson subscribers.

ARIZONA: *Boink!* A man who allegedly kidnapped a teenage girl and held her hostage briefly fought off police by throwing beer bottles at them. Police moving in to rescue the 14 year old runaway dodged the beer bottles and a flying chair before a swat team rescued her.

ARIZONA: *It appears that razor wire actually does work!* A jail inmate was left wearing nothing but his pink socks after scaling five fences in an attempt to escape before he was captured. The Maricopa County Sheriff's office spokesperson said Clayton Thornburg, 24, lost his jail uniform and underwear to razor wire in his failed escape attempt.

TEXAS: *Love, love, love makes them do such foolish things...* Houston police are on the lookout for a crazed stalker who twice rammed his car into the front entrance of a local TV station because he thought it would impress the traffic reporter. The reporter, Jennifer Reyna, of KPRC-TV had already taken out a restraining order on the man.

NEW MEXICO: *What, no time for a honeymoon???* Police in Albuquerque caught a prison parolee trying to flee to Mexico after he decided he did not want to take a drug test. With him was his fiancée. Police did not want to disappoint the love birds, so they arranged for a justice of the peace to come to the gas station where the pair had been stopped for a wedding ceremony where the groom wore handcuffs. Shortly after the ceremony the man was taken to jail.

CALIFORNIA: *My gosh, how hungry was she?* A woman at a Burbank McDonald's restaurant offered another customer sex in exchange for his Chicken McNuggets. He declined the offer. It is not certain whether he didn't want to part with his McNuggets or that she was just too ugly.

CALIFORNIA: *Geronimo...* A California porn star, who is also a skydiving instructor may be in for trouble. The porno skydiver was recently seen in a YouTube video posted online showing him jumping out of an airplane and having sex with a lady skydiver in midair. Police are still trying to discover whether Alex Torres' sex dive broke any law.

NEVADA: *Probably good the gun wasn't in his front pocket....*During a recent screening of the movie "The Bourne Legacy" at a Sparks' movie theater, a patron accidently shot himself in the buttocks when his weapon, for unknown reasons, went off in his pocket. He slowly stood up, apologized to his fellow moviegoers and went to the hospital. We learn he was not arrested, because he had a permit to carry the gun.

NEVADA: *You assume the risk of a broken window when you choose to live on a golf course, idiot!* A furious homeowner shot a golfer for slicing a golf ball through the homeowner's window near the 16th hole of a course in Reno. The golfer was not seriously injured, but we learn that the shooter will get more than a one stroke penalty. He is facing a felony assault rap.

ARIZONA: *The headline to the story simply read: "POT SHOT."* Mexican drug smugglers used powerful pneumatic cannons to propel more than 30 cans, each packed with 85 pounds of marijuana, over a border fence and into Arizona. "We've seen catapults but nothing like this," said Border Patrol spokesman Kyle Estes who said the Mary Jane was worth an estimated $42,000.

NEW MEXICO: *He must have TP'ed every house in Eastern New Mexico...* We discovered that Eastern New Mexico University recently received 80 rolls of toilet tissue along with an unsigned note from a person claiming to be a recent graduate apologizing for his ripping off that much tissue during his undergraduate days. The writer further admitted to have undergone a renewed dedication to Christianity and felt guilty about the petty "potty" theft.

TEXAS: *No chance this will ever pass – legislators love strip joints.* A lawmaker has proposed a law forcing all exotic dancers to be licensed – and to wear ID tags displaying their true names and license numbers while stripping. State Rep. Bill Zedler says he hopes the move will discourage women from entering the profession. It would at least guarantee that no "Amber" or "Aurora" or "Brandi" or "Chastity" or "Crystal" of "Destiny" or "Lola" mounts the pole in Texas again.

TEXAS: *Cynthia is a nincompoop...* Cynthia Creed, 51, had just been dismissed from jury duty in Houston when she texted a co-worker: "Call the courthouse. Tell them there is a bomb." Then, 15 minutes later she texted, "Just kidding." However, the co-worker had already called the police who evacuated the courthouse. Creed was arrested for giving a false police report.

TEXAS: *KA-POW, KA-POW, KA-POW....*Carrie King, 34, called Galveston police to report an intruder in her home. When police arrived they walked in on King furiously blasting away at Elvis Alexander, 53, with her paintball gun. Alexander was covered in yellow paint but was otherwise uninjured as police took him into custody.

ARIZONA: *Don't call us we'll call you....NOT!* Jobs are hard to come by in this economy. This lady went from bad to worse. The lady went to a home in Scottsdale to be interviewed for a position as a personal assistant and discovered the bodies of her two potential employers. Both of them had been shot to death.

TEXAS: *Yes, the police must make their quota of tickets!* Houston resident Natalie Plummer was arrested for holding up a sign alerting drivers to a speed trap. She did 12 hours in jail. Why? Police held her on an obscure charge of standing in the street where there's a sidewalk present – a misdemeanor.

TEXAS: *Here's one about a real life "Honest Abe."* We learn that a Houston man finally paid off his parking ticket from February 2, 1953. Abe Crawford, 79, dropped off his 1946 Nash automobile at a metered spot before shipping out to fight in Korea. His father was late in picking up the vehicle, leading to the ticket. Crawford had recently found the old, unpaid ticket in a box of keepsakes and arranged to pay the $1 fine.

ARIZONA: *"Shocked! I'm shocked that there is pot in there..." said the man."* *Dog turns up nose at paintings at the border!* A man taken into custody in Arizona after custom agents found 90 pounds of marijuana hidden in the frames of six large paintings in his vehicle. Agents picked the vehicle for a routine inspection at the border crossing in Douglas and their drug sniffing dog showed an immediate interest in the paintings. An X-ray revealed pot in the frames.

TEXAS: *Could this have been cruel and unusual punishment?* A Texas woman has filed a lawsuit in federal court. She is suing police for making her listen to Rush Limbaugh. Bridgett Nickerson was arrested in Harris County for driving on the shoulder of a highway in October 2010. While the sheriff's deputy drove her to jail, the car radio was broadcasting a Limbaugh show suing which Limbaugh allegedly made a "derogatory comments about black people," according to her filed court complaint. Boyd alleges that she is an African American.

ARIZONA: *Who Knew?* A chuckle headed football fan was fired from his dream job working at Super Bowl XLIX, after he posted a photo of himself flashing his credentials on Facebook. Russ Knight, who was hired to work on a radio broadcast, got a call from NFL security a few hours after he posted the photo of himself. Officials explained that they were firing him because it was against the rules to post photos of Super Bowl credentials online due to duplication concerns.

TEXAS: *No good deed goes unpunished...* This attorney did his job much too well! The offices of Jay Norton in San Antonio were burglarized by a man whom the attorney had just helped gain acquittal on a theft charge. In an ironic twist, the accused thief, Roger Ybarra, was a former police officer.

TEXAS: *Finders keepers' loser's weepers...* We learn that a group of handymen in El Paso got a $1 million bonus from a wall. They were knocking down the wall amid a home renovation when they hit the mother load with a sledgehammer. They, of course, turned over the money to the federal Drug Enforcement Agency, which is investigating.

For those of you who have never been there, El Paso is just across the Rio Grande from Ciudad Juarez, Mexico.

TEXAS: *Are there that many people looking to buy jails?* An insolvent Texas town solved its debt problem by selling its jail. A private prison firm paid $6 million for the Bill Clayton Detention Center in Littlefield, beating out two other bidders.

TEXAS: *Right! Double your pleasure, double your fun...* A Dallas driver was pulled over by police. The driver, knowing that there was an arrest warrant out for him on drug charges gave police his cousin's name instead of his true name. Bad move! The cousin was also wanted on an arrest warrant for alleged child molestation. However, it is reported that things worked out "doubly well" for the police. They got the driver and his cousin turned himself in after learning about his relative's arrest.

TEXAS: *Here's an ironic one.* An outlaw in Galveston saw an apparently empty auto near the beach and drove off with it. However, he soon realized a toddler was strapped in the back seat, he immediately drove back to where he had stolen the vehicle. He then hollered at the parents, warning them to never leave a child alone in a car...you never know when a thief may come along. No word whether he was caught by police. Ironic, huh!

ARIZONA: *D'Oh!* It appears that police in Glendale had little trouble finding fingerprints after copper wiring was stolen from a truck. While handling the wire, the thief severed a finger and left it at the scene of the crime.

TEXAS: *Deadbeats with no class!* Krystal G, 30, tried to stop a Dallas repo man from taking her car by tossing her one-year-old child into the back seat as he pulled away. Her 15-year-old son then shot the man in the leg with a 12 gauge shotgun. Ms. G and her son were arrested and the infant was taken into the custody of social services.

TEXAS: *Bessame Mucho. Some kiss...* We're sure she won't be kissed next year! A Dallas woman was arrested after biting her boyfriend's lower lip and tearing it off his face at midnight on New Year's Eve, police said. The victim did not want to punish Kerri Lyn Smith -- with whom he has a two year old son -- but she was still charge with aggravated assault.

TEXAS: *Shameful... Call her a real boob!* A trickster, Trista Joy Lathern, 24, faked having cancer and spent $10,000 raised at a benefit in her honor to get breast implants to salvage her seven-month marriage. Lathern, of Waco, was arrested and charged with theft by deception. Police said she shaved her head to look like she was going through chemotherapy, then had friends organize a benefit.

TEXAS: *Que estupido!* Police in Dallas are under fire for giving tickets to drivers who do not speak English. The rogue language enforcers were slapping violators with $204 fines, even though there is no law saying drivers must speak English. Police Chief David Kunkle said he will cancel the fines.

TEXAS: *Do not pray for what you want – you might get it!* Three people were injured at a church in Gilmer, as they prayed for a sign from God -- and an out of control driver slammed his SUV through the wall. The driver had accidentally hit the gas instead of the brake and ended up in the auditorium of the Zion Hill Baptist Church.

TEXAS: *That tool shed was one hell of a play pen!* A Texas couple was arrested after a state inspector found a half dozen children locked and unsupervised in a tool shed behind the unlicensed day care center. State officials said the children were surrounded by lawn equipment, gasoline and insecticide when they were found. The children were not injured. A child welfare inspector had gone there in response to a complaint that an illegal day care center was being operated at the home. In all there were 14 children, ranging in age from 3 months to 5 years, being cared for by the couple. Under Texas law they could only care for three children without a license.

TEXAS: *Bad Granny...* A Texas grandma will serve nine years in prison for drowning her 3 month old granddaughter in what her defense attorney said was a misguided effort to teach the baby to swim. Gabriella Sigler was watching little Melody Sigler in 2005 when she allegedly put her in a friend's pool. She had told her son earlier that she was teaching Melody to swim like she had seen on the TV show "water babies."

TEXAS: *Courtrooms can be such a "drag" some say.* A Texas defense attorney was arrested in a hall of justice for allegedly carrying marijuana and a pipe in her purse. A security guard at the Bexar County Courthouse arrested Regina Criswell, 50, at a screening station. The dopey legal eagle told authorities she had been holding the contraband for a client.

TEXAS: *Hey! Where do you think you are – at home?* Texas jailers shut down a jail facility that had turned into a basement lounge – with recliners in several cells and some prisoners having private locks on the doors of their home away from home. Others wrapped extension cords around bars as a means of keeping jailers out. The Texas Rangers finally put the clamps on the Montague county Jail, about 65 miles northwest of Fort Worth, and the inmates were shipped to nearby lockups.

TEXAS-MEXICO BORDER: *Dirty diapers anyone? Wonder what the chunky diapers smelled like? Phew....* U.S. Customs inspectors on the border discovered several links of spicy chorizo sausage hidden inside some chunky diapers whose owner, a 21 year old woman, said they were merely soiled. You can't do this! Taking certain agricultural products – including sausages – across the

U.S. border is illegal. The woman was fined $300.

TEXAS: *Talk about low lifes…stealing preacher's wallet. "Thou shalt not steal" might have been a better sermon.* A preacher's wallet was stolen by two thieves who went on a shopping spree around Fort Worth, while he delivered a sermon on showing mercy to others. The pair ran up $2,000 in purchases on the Rev. Rob Hamby's credit cards. "What troubles me is that they would go to the church, not to help but to steal," Hamby said. "I am shocked and frustrated."

TEXAS: *Tsk, tsk, too young to be a designated driver.* In mid-August, 2008, a 35 year old Houston woman was arrested after she made her 12 year old daughter drive her to a bar outside Houston. Police spotted the obviously unlicensed girl driving erratically. She told police she had dropped off her mom who was afraid to drive drunk.

NEW MEXICO: *True That...* Descendants of legendary old west lawman Pat Garrett have urged New Mexico's governor to reject a plan to posthumously pardon Billy the Kid. The notorious outlaw was killed in 1881 by Garrett, whose relatives contend such a move would tarnish their ancestor's honor. One of them, Pauline Garrett Tillinghast, said, "We have a tendency unfortunately in this country to glorify criminals."

ARIZONA: *We have never heard of the charge of "giving a false impression of a terrorist act." It sounds silly...* A Phoenix man allegedly dressed his 16 year old nephew in a sheet and had him carry a fake grenade launcher in the streets, all to test police response time. Mitchell Turnblat, 49, was charged with giving a false impression of a terrorist act, endangerment, contributing to the delinquency of a minor and misconduct involving a simulated explosive. We learn it took police 15 minutes for police to respond.

ARIZONA: *This was not like Native Americans using psychotropic drugs to get closer to God.* A minister was recently arrested for allegedly selling parishioners heroin, meth and prescription drugs. However, Michael Benjamin, pastor of Faith Mountain Christian Church, maintains that he was only slinging the drugs to "bring them closer to God," according to the Maricopa County Sheriff Joe Arpaio.

NEW MEXICO: *Yes, Carlos, life is tough on the streets.* Convict Carlos Garcia spent five months hacking away at the bars of his cell window with a razor blade taped to a Popsicle stick until he finally cut through and escaped. But as soon as he got out he changed his mind and climbed back inside. He is now serving the remainder of his life sentence in solitary confinement.

NEW MEXICO: *"Cold case." We get it! Cops can be such comedians...* One fine day a worker in a supermarket in Roswell opened a case of frozen ribs, and, to his surprise, he discovered a handgun and ammunition packed amid the meat. Police traced the meat to a packing plant in Greely, Colorado and police there are trying to determine whether the weapon was used in any cold case.

NEW MEXICO: *Insane or just mad?* You've heard about Kung-Fu fighting. How about Kung-Fu driving? Beverly Moore, 36, of Carlsbad was arrested for allegedly swinging nun chucks from the sunroof of her car and failing to stop. A 65 mph chase ended when police laid down spike strips. She was taken to a hospital for a mental evaluation.

ARIZONA: *He sounds like the Galloping Ghost...*A slick talking Arizona man has managed to escape from jails in two states by pretending to be other inmates. Rocky Delgado Marquez, 34, was arrested in 2010 on DWI forgery and other charges, but got away from an Arizona jail in May 2011 by convincing jailers he was a different inmate. He spent eight months on the lam and was arrested in Detroit. He was being held pending extradition, but allegedly escaped again in 2012 using the same scam.

THE END

About the Author

Professor Birdsong received his J.D. from the Harvard Law School and his B.A. from Howard University. He teaches law in Orlando, Florida.

After graduation from law school he worked four years at the law firm of Baker Hostetler. He then entered into a varied and distinguished career in government service. He served as a diplomat with the U.S. State Department with various postings in Nigeria, Germany and the Bahamas.

Professor Birdsong later served as a federal prosecutor. After leaving government service, and before he began teaching, Professor Birdsong was in private law practice in Washington, D.C.

www.BirdsongsLaw.com

lbirdsong@barry.edu

Ordering Information

New books coming soon!

Dear Reader,

If you liked this book, I would greatly appreciate you writing me a review on Amazon or any other book site.

I look forward to sharing more funny stories with you in future books.

Thank you, I really appreciate your help.

Regards,

Professor Birdsong

Winghurst Publications
1969 S. Alafaya Trail / Suite 303
Orlando, FL 32828-8732
www.BirdsongsLaw.com
lbirdsong@barry.edu

Books by Professor Birdsong

* Professor Birdsong's 147 Dumbest Criminal Stories: Florida

* Professor Birdsong's 117 Dumbest Criminal Stories: The Southwest

* 177 Dumbest Criminal Stories – International

* Professor Birdsong's 157 Dumbest Criminal Stories

* Professor Birdsong's *BEST!* 207 Dumbest and Weird Criminal Stories

* Professor Birdsong's Weird Criminal Law Stories

* Professor Birdsong's "365" Weird Criminal Law Stories for Every Day of the Year

* Professor Birdsong's Weird Criminal Law Stories, Volume 2: Stories From Around the States and Abroad

* Professor Birdsong's Weird Criminal Law Stories, Volume 3: Stories from New York City and the East Coast

* Professor Birdsong's Weird Criminal Law Stories - Volume 4: Stories from the Midwest

* Professor Birdsong's Weird Criminal Law Stories, Volume 5: Stories from Way Out West

* Professor Birdsong's Weird Criminal Law Stories - Volume 6: Women in Trouble

* Professor Birdsong's Weird Criminal Law - Volume 6: Women in Trouble!

* Immigration: Obama must act now!

www.ingramcontent.com/pod-product-compliance
Lightning Source LLC
Chambersburg PA
CBHW071849020426
42331CB00007B/1922